Pucks, Sticks, and DIAPERS

Pucks, Sticks, and DIAPERS

An awesome short story of
Jayden and Baylor Sinclair

TONI ALEO

Interior Design and Formatting by:

www.emtippettsbookdesigns.com

Sleeping with a Pregnant Woman

"Babe."

"Hm?

"Hey, can you scoot over?"

"I'm on the edge."

His brows coming in, Jayden Sinclair looked over his shoulder, right into the face of his sleeping wife. "Babe, I find that hard to believe."

"Huh?"

"There is no way you're on the edge when your knee is up under my balls, the other leg is over my hip, and your nose is in my shoulder—while our child is kicking me to death in my back."

Grumbling, Baylor said, "But I am."

"You're not."

"You scoot over."

"Bay, I'm on the edge of our California King bed that you said we had to have so we didn't touch during the night because you always get so hot, and I'm a furnace. But yet, you're basically on top of me."

1

"I am not," she complained, nuzzling closer, as if that were possible. "Shh, go to sleep."

Sighing loudly, he glared at the wall. "I can't because, this time, you're the furnace, and like I said, our child is kicking me."

"You're welcome for giving you a preview of my life," she said in his ear on an exhale. "Can you stop talking? I'm tired."

Usually, he wouldn't care. He'd deal with it because he loved her and wanted her to be comfortable. Lord knew, this pregnancy hadn't been easy. At first, Baylor had been recovering from her painful knee surgery without pain meds once they found out she was carrying. The surprise of a child was a little more than they had been ready for. He had been knee-deep in hockey, working hard for the final prize, while Baylor was dealing with the fact that her career was over. After becoming the first woman in the NHL, Baylor hadn't expected ever to quit, but injury led to that. She was ready to start working, at what she wasn't sure since she had never had any plans beyond hockey, but then the surprise of a child rattled their world.

Especially when neither of them had discussed ever having kids.

It wasn't in the cards. Hockey was in the cards, and that was it. But Jayden's mom, Autumn, had always said, "The best surprises are those that knock you on your ass." Well, hearing Baylor was pregnant sure knocked him on his ass. And her on hers.

But after the initial shock, they both became beyond excited.

Or so they thought. Because weeks after she started feeling like a person again and not an invalid, then she got godawful sick. Baylor had lost over ten pounds, and for a while there, Jayden was nervous because of how skinny she looked. She couldn't eat without throwing up, and she wouldn't take medicine because she was so nervous for the health of the baby. She was still nervous that the pain meds she had taken when she was injured could have hurt the baby, and she didn't want to cause any more problems for their child. While he agreed with the doctors, there was no arguing with a passionate Baylor. So

instead, she puked her brains out, and he couldn't do anything but watch and hand her crackers.

But then, by the grace of God, she started eating again without throwing up. He hadn't realized he could get so excited or turned on watching his wife eat two slabs of steak, a hot dog, two portions of potato salad, and beans. He was just thankful, happy, and optimistic for their future. Hockey was going great, the Assassins were playing the best he had seen them play in a while, but nothing could compare to the moment their child started to show itself in his wife's belly.

Jayden was convinced he had fallen in love with her all over again.

Months passed, the baby grew, and they decided not to find out what it was when the time came. They had decided since the baby was a surprise from the beginning, it should stay that way. He was thrilled. Though, he felt in his heart it was a boy. Jayden couldn't explain it, but he just felt it and that filled him with all the excitement imaginable. He already had two nieces, and he knew he would have the first grandson. Just knew it.

Baylor was doing well too. She wasn't sick, she was walking well, and she actually felt normal again. She had gone to work with her dad as the assistant coach for the boys hockey team over at Bellevue University, where she and Jayden had both graduated from. They were happy, things were good. But then the baby moved onto Baylor's sciatic nerve. While he loved watching his baby grow, he hated seeing Baylor in pain. It would paralyze her—to the point where she would need to sit down and wait for the baby to move.

Jayden was convinced Baylor hated life, but when he asked, she assured him she had never been happier.

He was now always two seconds from a panic attack.

His constant worry for her was maddening, but then he had the Assassins to worry for too. They were in the play-offs, kicking ass, but they couldn't close. Losing at the end. It was heartbreaking. He wanted more than anything to hold that Cup up. But then he realized he was about to hold his baby, and that was an even greater prize.

That was, if he didn't kill Baylor first.

Turning over, she glared at him as he sat up on his arm, looking over her to the amount of space beside her. "Baylor, we could fit the whole team beside you."

Her brows came in even more. "What are you saying?"

"I'm saying, scoot the hell over!" he said, his voice rising. "You're burning me up!"

"I want to sleep with you."

"You are, but give me some space so I don't die of heatstroke!"

With a grunt of annoyance, she rolled over. "Ugh, whatever."

Shaking his head, Jayden lay down once more, cuddling into his pillow. He could breathe. But just as he started to fall asleep, though, she said, "I just think it's messed up that you won't cuddle with me and I'm carrying your child, which is the reason I'm burning up."

Opening his eyes, he stared at the wall.

And here they went.

"Babe, I love cuddling with you. But I have to be up early to clean out my locker and do press. I can't sleep through that, and I definitely can't sleep with you burning me up and our child kicking the hell out of me." He looked over his shoulder at her and smiled. "I love you, though. You know that, right?"

But she was glaring, her little lips pursed as she held his gaze. "Oh yeah, I forgot you live such a busy life and need all the sleep you get. While I can't sleep a certain way due to the fact it hurts because I'm the vessel your child is sucking the life out of."

"I thought you loved being pregnant."

"I do!" she yelled, and his brows went up. "That's not the point. I'm just reminding you that I don't get sleep, and I sure as hell don't get to play hockey anymore, but it's fine. I'll *try* to sleep all the way over here, alone and without the love and support of my husband because *he* has to get some sleep. God forbid he doesn't have sleep," she mumbled, and he wanted to laugh. She was ridiculous. But before he could tell her that, she looked over at him and said, "And just a reminder, Jayden Sinclair, when this child comes, say fucking good-bye to sleep."

Blinking, he held her gaze. "I guess I should say good-bye to sleep now because I'm sure I'm not getting any more tonight."

Her eyes darkened, and he swore he had never seen anyone as beautiful as his wife. Even with her hostility, he thought she was gorgeous. That may have made him an insane man, but he didn't care. "You got that right," she snapped, rolling over and letting out a loud sigh. "I just wanted to cuddle."

When he heard her sniff, he closed his eyes, a smile pulling at his lips. The emotional roller coaster of Baylor Sinclair was a ride no man should ever have to experience, but Jayden was in the front-row seat. Reaching out, he went to cuddle with her, but she smacked him away. "I don't want to cuddle now!"

"Fine," he said, rolling over and cuddling back into the pillows. Sometimes, he couldn't win with her.

"I just want you to know, I did want to cuddle, but that's gone now!"

"I hear you."

"And I'm upset!"

"I got that," he said with a sigh as he slowly back rolled over, looking at her.

"I don't think it's fair. I cook, I clean, I work, and by the way, I'm carrying your child!"

"And I appreciate you more than I can ever say."

"Then you'd cuddle with me!"

"But, Bay, I need sleep as much as you do, and you are giving off the heat of Mordor," he tried, but she shook her head, glaring at him.

"Well, if you need sleep and I'm so hot and our child won't stop kicking you, then go sleep somewhere else!"

"Seriously?"

"Yes! Go to the couch!"

Surely, she was joking. But then she yanked the covers off him, pulling his pillow out from under him and throwing it to the floor. "I need sleep, and I'm too mad at you to sleep with you in here. So, you go."

"Because I won't cuddle with you?"

"Yes," she yelled, the tears rolling down her face.

"Then come here, I'll cuddle," he tried, but she threw the covers to the floor.

"No! I don't want to cuddle!"

"Then let's go to bed."

"No! I'm mad!"

"You're being ridiculous," he laughed, and why in the world he did that would be his last thought.

Because he was pretty sure he was about to die.

"*Go!*" she roared, at which he paused.

He was waiting for her head to start spinning.

When it didn't, though, he held her gaze. "If I go, I'm not coming back tonight."

"That's fine. Maybe tomorrow you won't mind cuddling with your child and wife."

"Baylor, I said, let's cu—"

"I don't want to cuddle," she yelled, falling into the bed with a sob. "I just wanted you to want to cuddle with me!"

Watching as she cried, he slowly shook his head. They obviously needed some time apart, or better yet, he needed to go to give her time to breathe. Getting out of bed, he picked up his blankets and pillows and then looked back down to her. "You sure?"

"Did I stutter?" she snapped, pulling the blankets up to her face. "You broke my heart, Jayden."

He went to say something snarky, but he knew it would get him nowhere. "I'm sorry for the fact I didn't want to cuddle because of the death heat you were putting off. I love you. Good night."

When she didn't answer, he shook his head, smiling as he walked out of the room. Heading to the couch, he lay down and looked up at the ceiling. Only two more months, and then maybe he'd get his sane wife back. He was lucky he played on a team with men who had kids and also had gone through the months of torture otherwise known as pregnancy. If not, he wouldn't know it was normal for his wife to be completely and utterly irrational about the stupidest things.

Today, it was cuddling.

A week ago, it was because he ate the last Oreo.

Next week, it might because he moved something she needed.

Lord, two more months. He could make it.

Leaning back on the pillow, he slowly closed his eyes, thankful he'd chosen the most comfortable couch known to man. He hoped she had stopped crying. He was tempted to check, but he really didn't want her to bite his head off. Cuddling into the pillows, he rolled to his side, and just as he was about to drift away, he felt someone beside him.

Opening his eyes, he saw his very pregnant wife looking down at him.

She looked adorable, her hair a mess, her shorts way too short and too tight. The shirt she wore was one she used to wear when they were in college. A crop top that now made her look more like Winne the Pooh than the young girl with her heart set on playing in the NHL. He was pretty sure Winnie had nothing on his hot, sexy wife, though, who was still crying.

"Jayden?"

"Yeah, babe?"

"Can I lie with you?"

He didn't want to fight with her. He wanted to love her, but sometimes, she made that so damn difficult. Chuckling to himself, he scooted over as far as he could as she lay beside him, her stomach pressing hard into his as she wrapped her arms around his neck, kissing his jaw.

"I'm sorry I'm batshit crazy," she whispered against his cheek, her tears wetting his face. Their child moved like mad, kicking against him, and all he could do was hug her back.

"It's okay, baby," he answered, kissing her once more.

"I love you," she whispered back, her heart pounding into his.

"And I love you, babe. Go to sleep."

"Okay."

And as she cuddled into him, he knew he'd wake up sorer than hell and maybe even a little grumpy, but it would be okay.

Because he was in love with the most difficult woman on the planet, and she loved him back.

BBQ at the Adlers

"We're so glad y'all could come!"

Looking to her husband, Baylor found herself breathless at the grin that covered Jayden's face as his boss, Elli Adler, gathered her in her arms. "Don't you look amazing! I love it!" she gushed, cupping Baylor's growing belly as she looked to Jayden. "You did good, Mr. Sinclair."

Looking down at herself, Baylor thought she looked crazy for the simple fact it looked as if her kid was completely sprawled out instead of being in a ball inside of her. But who was she to judge? She still had no clue what was going on; this pregnancy thing was one scary feat, but she was almost to the finish line. She almost had her prize.

"Isn't she gorgeous?" Jayden asked, kissing her cheek. Still, even after two years of marriage, she felt like it was all a dream. She'd always known that they had something special and that he was the man for her, even thought she'd tried to deny it. Really, who finds their soul mate at twenty-one? She did, and she thanked her lucky stars for him. They were so happy. Even when she got injured and her career ended early, she was still happy.

Because he made her happy.

Not too many men would even try to love her, but Jayden did it with the passion of a thousand armies. Lord knew, she wasn't easy to deal with before the pregnancy, but now, with their child in her, she had the mood swings of thirty sixteen-year-old girls on their periods. She gave him a hard time about almost everything, yet he loved her through it. More than she could ever deserve.

"She is. Come in, come in," Elli said, ushering them inside.

Baylor loved coming to the Adler home. It was so full of love. The walls were decorated with the most unbelievably gorgeous photos of the Adler clan. Baylor was particularly jealous of the amazing wedding photos of Elli and her husband, Shea, that covered the walls. Baylor and Jayden hadn't had a fancy wedding because they eloped after they were both drafted into the NHL, but sometimes, Baylor wished she had. She didn't want the big puffy dress and all the hoopla, but she wanted the pictures. They had nothing from their wedding. Just the paper.

But she couldn't dwell on that, not when all the little faces of the Adler clan looked out at her from the various stages of their lives. The five Adler kids were just as famous as their parents to some. Each had a personality that shone as bright as their smiles in the pictures. Baylor had a special place in her heart for the oldest Adler, Shelli. For the simple fact that girl would make it in the NHL one day.

Or on Broadway. Something. She was amazing.

"I love your house, Elli," Baylor said as they headed through the house and kitchen to the backyard, where Shea and the kids were swimming.

"Thank you, lots of love in this house for sure. Shea wants to get a bigger one, but I can't let it go. Not yet, maybe when the kids are bigger, or when the boys burn it down," Elli explained with a laugh. "Lord help us all when that happens," she added, and Baylor laughed as Jayden's fingers threaded with hers.

"Or them," Jayden laughed, and she nodded.

"Right, skin their hides for sure," she agreed with a grin, and Baylor smiled.

Elli loved her children more than she loved herself. She was strict, but she was a great mom.

"We'll need a bigger one when we have more," he said, and Baylor laughed.

"*If* we have any more. This pregnancy has not been easy," she said with a sigh, and they both nodded, knowing it hadn't. Not even kind of, and with Elli being a close friend, she knew all about it, always offering a lot of help and knowledge.

"It will all be worth it, don't worry. Plus, if the pregnancy is tough, usually, the baby is easier."

"Is that true, or are you lying to us to get through the last several weeks?" Jayden asked, his lips curving, and that made them all laugh.

"I'm lying," she teased, opening the patio door just as Shea jumped into the pool, sending the kids into a fit of laughter. Shelli, Posey, Owen, Evan, and Quinn all sat on the edge, cheering their father as he came up sputtering.

"That was easily a ten," he called out to them, but Quinn shook his head.

"No, Dad, you didn't tuck in hard enough."

"And your legs weren't together," Owen added.

"Plus, your splash was too big," Posey included, and Shea wasn't impressed.

"It was supposed to be big. I'm the winner," he grumbled, to which all the kids protested.

"They've been watching a lot of swimming competitions on TV," Elli said as she pulled out a chair for Baylor and then yelled to her family. "Baylor and Jayden are here!"

The kids whipped around, getting up to say hi and for hugs, more so for Jayden than Baylor, though. They all loved him, probably because he played with them more than she did. She didn't let that bother her, though; she knew he was better with kids than she was. It made her a bit nervous since she was having a kid, but with how great Jayden was, she knew she'd catch on.

"Come swim with us, Jay," Evan begged, but Elli shook her head, moving his dark brown hair out of his eyes before pushing his goggles up his nose.

11

"Y'all go on. We're having adult time, then the guys will come," she said, and though the kids groaned their dismay, they all ran off, jumping into the pool like little Olympic divers.

"About to pop there, Sinclair," Shea said as he came over, kissing Baylor's cheek before reaching for his towel to dry off.

"Not soon enough," she laughed, and he smiled as he sat down beside her.

Jayden sat on the other side beside Elli and nodded. "You can say that again," he teased, and she glared playfully, at which he kissed her loudly on the lips. "Not that I haven't loved every second of this pregnancy—or the sleepless nights," he quipped. She knew he was speaking of the night the previous week. She never claimed to be sane, especially with this pregnancy. Sometimes she didn't even know the Preggosauras that was roaring through the house.

"You shouldn't be having sleepless nights yet," Shea laughed, and Jayden nodded.

"Tell that to my lovely wife," he laughed, and Baylor's face burned.

"He wouldn't cuddle with me," she complained to Elli. "And I got mad, kicked him out of bed, and then I went to lie down with him on the couch."

Elli looked to Jayden and shook her head. "You jerk, I'm benching you," she teased, which sent everyone into gales of laughter. Benching the captain of the Assassins? Yeah, that wouldn't happen.

"True friend there," Baylor laughed, and Elli sent her a grin.

Shaking his head, Jayden took Elli's shoulder, laughing. "So instead, we slept on a couch one-fourth the size of our bed. I had a backache, but she was happy."

"Okay, I won't bench you," she decided, and Baylor grinned.

"So are you excited for the baby shower? Only a couple weeks, right?"

"You mean the humongous shindig my mother-in-law is planning? Yes, I'm ready for it to be over," Baylor said with a grin for her husband.

Baby showers were supposed to be small, cute, and painless, but apparently, Autumn Sinclair didn't get that memo. This was the first baby shower she was

able to plan since, with her first two grandchildren, she hadn't been asked. But Baylor's dad thought it would bring them closer as a family if Baylor asked his wife, who was also Baylor's mother-in-law, to plan it. She didn't mind, she loved Autumn, but she wasn't sure this was the way to bring them closer. If anything, it was going to drive them apart because they did not need jugglers at a baby shower.

"The invites were fancy," Elli giggled, her eyes playful, and Baylor glared.

"She wanted to make it a circus theme with elephants," Baylor complained, and Jayden laughed.

"My mom is excited, obviously."

"As she should be. Babies are exciting!" Elli cheered, clapping her hands.

"Why so late, though? Aren't you due like a week later?" Shea asked, and Baylor grinned.

"You know my due date?"

He gave her a deadpan look. "It's circled on the calendar because my wife is OCD."

Laughing as Elli glared at her husband, Baylor nodded. "It's two weeks out. Everyone will be in for the dress fitting for Lucy's wedding, so Autumn wanted to do it that weekend to coordinate," she said and let out a long breath, feeling the pressure.

Too much was going on, in her opinion. Weddings, babies, hockey season, it was a lot, yet somehow, she was surviving. She chalked it all up to Jayden, though. She couldn't do half of what she did without him. The nights when she was in such pain and he would massage her back or legs. Or when he held her hair as she puked her guts out, always on standby with crackers. He was amazing. They argued, but they had always argued. It was their foreplay, but nothing was ever serious enough to hurt each other.

Thankfully.

"Dress fitting?" Elli asked, smiling. "Pregnant?"

"Exactly. I'm the size of a house, but I'm being forced to go."

13

"It will be fine. You'll be gorgeous," Jayden said, ever so reassuring.

"That wedding is going to be an affair too! I saw all the awesome stuff when we went to Grace's house last week. I bet Lucy and Benji are excited," Elli said, speaking of Shea's sister, who was also the wedding planner for Lucy and Benji.

"Yeah, it's going to be something," Jayden laughed, shaking his head. "I hate that the season got pushed back, though. I'm ready to get back."

"Yeah, but with Worlds, we had no choice. No biggie, gives us time to fix the holes we've got." Elli decided with a nod, and she wasn't kidding. They had traded a lot of players, brought in a few new ones, and even had some good draft choices. The puck was in Elli's zone, and it was her time to put together a winning team.

"We need a strong D for me since your husband retired," Jayden said to his old defense partner. "You drafted a great one, by the way."

Elli nodded, holding his gaze. "Markus Reeves?"

"Yup, he's great."

"He is, very strong player," Baylor added, and Elli shrugged, pressing her lips together.

"They don't like him down in Florida, did you know?" she said then, and Jayden's face changed to surprise. Even Baylor was shocked by that. Markus, who was her best friend and a family friend to the Sinclairs, was one of the greatest guys and players she knew. How anyone couldn't like him or his game was unfathomable to her. Markus was wonderful.

"Really? He's great."

"He hasn't impressed," she said. Baylor hated that. She'd have to call him, tell him to get his shit together. He had to get into the NHL; she was rooting for him.

"Maybe he needs a good coach to play for. St. Marc is a douche," Jayden said, speaking of the coach of the Assassins' farm team, the Ninjas.

"Maybe," Elli agreed and then looked toward the pool as the kids screamed and played. "I'll consider it."

"You should. He's one of the best players I know," Baylor said, reaching out to touch the petals of the arrangement of tulips that sat in the middle of the table. They were artificial. Laughing, she said, "I thought they were real."

Elli grinned. "It's the replica of my bouquet from my wedding. Since mine were real, they gave me this to keep forever."

"How nice," Baylor cooed, her lips curving. "I wish we had something from our wedding."

"We have each other," Jayden suggested, and Baylor shrugged.

"We do, but maybe we should have a wedding," she suggested, and his brow rose. "For pictures and faux flower arrangements."

He eyed her. "Is this part of the emotional roller coaster, or is this real?"

Elli and Shea both laughed as Baylor held his gaze. "Really?"

"What? I never know!" he protested, and she glared.

"He doesn't take me seriously. Ever," she said to Elli then, and Jayden laughed.

"I do too. I just never know what is real and what is emotional!"

"Welcome to the rest of your life," Shea said before he was rewarded with a smack from his wife.

"Don't listen to him, and I think a wedding is a great idea," she cheered, trying to change the subject, but Baylor was still glaring at her husband.

"I don't like you."

"But you want to marry me?"

"Yes," she said, holding his gaze.

With a grin, he nodded. "See what I mean?" he said to Shea, flashing her a full grin. "But, okay then, we'll have a wedding."

"Yay! I'll plan it," Elli exclaimed, but Shea groaned.

"When? You own an NHL team, are raising kids, and have to love me. I'm needy, woman," Shea demanded, and that had Baylor sputtering with laughter while Elli rolled her eyes.

Before she could argue with her husband, though, Jayden interjected,

"We'll revisit this later. Let's have our kiddo first."

Baylor shared a look with her husband and then nodded. "Sounds good to me."

"Yay, I can't wait!" Elli leaned into her husband, who was looking at her like she owned his world. And Baylor guessed she did; they were what every couple wanted to be. Everyone loved the Adlers, and boy, did they love each other.

"Jay, can you play with us? Daddy, come on," Shelli said then, pulling Baylor's attention to where all the kids stood, dripping with water but still holding their hockey sticks.

"Now?" Jayden asked, laughing, but he was already standing, taking the stick Posey held out to him. "Yeah, let's go. You're going down, Shea."

"Please, I'm going to ruin you," Shea said, taking the stick Owen was offering.

"Okay," Jayden laughed as he kissed Baylor's forehead.

"Hey, I want to play," she said, slowly getting up, but he stopped her.

"No, you stay here, talk woman stuff," he said, kissing her once more.

"But I want to beat you," she complained as she rolled her eyes at his comment. "You know I can."

That really had him laughing. "Please."

Getting up, she took his stick and challenged, "Wanna see?"

While she could see the competitive need to beat her in his eyes, she also saw a flicker of worry. "You don't need to be running around with your knee still healing. Plus, I don't want you to get hit in the belly. But afterward, it's on."

Holding his gaze, she knew he was right, but she wanted to play.

It was obvious he didn't want to fight as he sighed. "I don't want you to get hurt, baby. So we'll shake on it now that, once you're ready, we go to the rink, and then we can watch me kick your ass."

Glaring at him, she scoffed. "You mean, me kicking your ass," she corrected, handing him back the stick and holding her hand out. "It's on."

Taking her hand, he shook it before kissing her hard on the lips. "You're going down."

"Yeah, okay," she teased as she lowered back into the seat, and the kids all dragged him off to play.

Looking to Elli, Baylor found her friend shaking her head. "You will always be the most fearless and headstrong woman I know," Elli said and then laughed. "I love it, though."

"Thank God he does too." Baylor smiled as she watched the kids play with Shea and Jayden.

As Jayden cut left around Owen to go right around Evan, he shot, only to miss the goal, and she smiled. While she would have made that, she knew she had picked a great man to love, to marry, and then get pregnant by.

Now she just needed the baby to come so she would have the perfect life she never knew she always wanted.

Lucy & Benji are getting married!

"**W**hy am I here?"

Baylor's sister-in-law Avery, who was married to Jayden's baby brother, Jace, looked over at her and shrugged. "Because Lucy is mean."

With Avery's daughter, Ashlyn, on her hip, Jayden's big sister, Lucy, glared. "I am not. This is a family affair. We all have to be here and enjoy it. Love each other and encourage each other as we go through this. Because what would my wedding be without my beautiful and amazing sisters-in-law?"

Baylor scoffed as Avery laughed. "Mom told you to say that?"

Lucy nodded. "Yes. I hate this and want to go home."

"You do not," Autumn cooed, coming over and kissing her granddaughter's cheek. "You love it! And Baylor, sweetheart, even though the dress doesn't fit you now, we have to make sure you like it."

"Mom, we all hate the dresses," Claire, Baylor's other sister-in-law, who was married to Jayden's older brother, Jude, said as she wrapped her arm across their mother-in-law's shoulders. "It's a bridesmaid dress. No one ever likes their bridesmaid dresses."

18

"That's true. Yours was ugly as hell," Lucy said, and Claire agreed.

"I love them all. Now hush, all of you, because my sweet little baby girl is coming out in her precious little dress," Autumn exclaimed, going to the podium as Lucy's daughter, Angie, walked up in her junior bridesmaid dress. It was a soft, baby-blue color that brought out the blue that flaked in her green eyes. Her brown hair was a mess on top of her head, but no one could stop the grin on her little face.

"I'm a bridesmaid!" Angie cheered, and everyone grinned.

"Yup, and the prettiest one ever," Autumn gushed, kissing her cheeks.

"Hey!" Claire, Avery, and Baylor all said jokingly together as Lucy laughed.

"I can't wait," Angie said, grinning up at her mother and grandmother as they asked for things to be tightened and shortened here and there.

As Baylor watched, she held her belly, rubbing it until Claire came over, pressing her hand into Baylor's bump. "Is it moving? Aw, it is!" Claire giggled, and Baylor smiled.

"It's always moving. It's awesome." It really was; it was her favorite part of her pregnancy…until it got on her nerve. Then she was in hell.

"Doesn't it drive you crazy not knowing what it is?" Avery asked, placing her hand on Baylor's belly. "I needed to say he or she. I had to know."

Baylor shrugged. "Nope, I'm excited for the big day. To finally find out."

"Well, it kills me not knowing!" Lucy said, playfully glaring back at her. "I don't know if I should buy a suit or a dress for them. And if it's not a boy, I won't have a ring bearer."

"That's fine, Ashlyn and the new baby can do both. Plus, no one cares. They're there to make people go awwwww," Avery said, drawing it out as she tickled Ashlyn, who giggled loudly for her mommy.

"And you know everyone will," Claire said, taking Ashlyn from Lucy and kissing her cheek. "Or at least, I will."

Baylor smiled. "You're next, Claire."

She laughed. "Nope, not ready. See, we know about this thing called birth control, and we use it," she teased, and everyone laughed.

"Hey, I was on it!" Baylor called to her as Claire grinned back at her.

"That's what they all say."

"Not me. I wasn't, and we had faulty condoms," Avery said with a snort, which sent them all into fits of laughter. "But I wouldn't change a thing," she said, grinning at her little girl.

Baylor couldn't wait to feel that way because at that moment, she was rethinking ever getting pregnant again.

"Yeah, so watch out for faulty birth control and condoms," Baylor warned, and Claire waved them off.

"Duly noted, but until I'm back with Jude full time in Los Angeles, we aren't having any babies. It would just be too hard on us," she said, and Baylor nodded. They had been apart for a couple years now, with Claire's job in Vegas and Jude playing for the Kings, but it had worked. They were more in love than Baylor ever thought they could be, but she also knew Autumn was waiting for her oldest boy to have a baby. Autumn Sinclair was all about babies, hence the out-of-control baby shower she was planning.

"Plus, we all know everyone is waiting for Benji and Lucy to have a baby," Claire said, and Lucy scoffed at her.

"Whoa, no. We don't have time."

"Yes, you do," Avery said, and Lucy laughed.

"And so do you. Why don't you have another?"

Avery giggled hard at that. "No, I don't! I'm currently working with an awesome songwriter for Selena Gomez. Plus, we're waiting until we can drink legally before we add in another."

"You'll need it," Autumn agreed, and that had everyone in stitches.

"Okay, girls, go try your dresses on," Autumn called, and when everyone got up, Baylor stayed in her seat.

They looked back at her, and she shrugged. "What? I could maybe get it up my thighs, but even I'm not sure on that. So I'm good."

"Party pooper," Claire teased.

"Yeah, who told you to get pregnant when we had a wedding coming up?" Avery added, and Baylor snorted.

"Aren't they already married?" Baylor asked, and that made them both grin as they headed toward where Autumn and the salesperson were waiting for them.

Looking around the cute little shop, Baylor had a smile on her face as she rubbed her belly. While there was no point for her to be there, she was glad she was. She loved her sisters-in-law, along with her stepmother slash mother-in-law. Add in Angie and Ashlyn, and Baylor was in heaven. Growing up with only her dad, she had yearned for a big family like the one she had now. Yeah, they were all crazy, but God, she loved them. She couldn't wait for her little bundle to join them.

It would be complete bliss.

When her eyes met a section of the store with a sign that read Maternity, she found herself getting up and heading toward it. Looking through the dresses, she thought they were adorable, and a part of her wished she needed one. She didn't, though.

"Oh, Baylor, I forgot to tell you," Autumn said, coming over to Baylor and rubbing her back. "Lord, I'm losing it. Anyway, pick one."

Baylor's face scrunched up. "What?"

"Pick one of these dresses. I want you to look amazing at the baby shower. I hired a photographer."

"Mom…" Baylor said in complete disbelief. This woman was insane. It was a baby shower, not a damn wedding.

"Yes?"

"You're serious?"

"Yes."

"For the love of…" she muttered, looking through the dresses. "But they're all wedding dresses!"

"So?"

"They're also expensive!"

"Again, so?"

Rolling her eyes, Baylor picked a few before waddling to the dressing room because the simple fact was there was no arguing with Autumn Sinclair. She tried on two that were too tight on her ever-growing belly, and when she went to try on the third, she paused. Scoffing, she drank in her body and shook her head. She would never look the same ever again. The baby was huge, and her usually very fit body was stretched to hell. Dark purple and red marks ran up her sides and along her thighs. She hadn't eaten badly during her pregnancy, she had taken care of herself, but her little person decided it didn't have enough room. She wondered if she even had abs anymore.

But she guessed that was a part of motherhood.

Sighing loudly, she reached for the third dress, a beautiful, off-white lace number, but before she could pull it over her bump, her phone rang. It was Jayden.

"Hey."

"Hey, you guys done?"

"Nope, your mother is making me pick out a dress for the baby shower."

He laughed. "She's crazy."

"Exactly my thought," she said on a sigh. "Oh, and by the way, I'm disgusting naked. How do you still wanna do me?"

"What's disgusting? What are you talking about?"

"My body is ruined."

"Your body is fucking hot, and I love it, so stop talking about it."

"But it is."

"No, it's not. Shut up, I love that body," he demanded. "I'm getting hard just thinking about that curve of your ass. The thickness of those sexy thighs and God, those tits, mmm, yeah… When are you coming home?"

As her face turned red, she let out a little giggle. "Jay, be real. I'm covered in stretch marks."

"And? They mean you grew my child, and again, I think that's hot."

"You're insane."

"About you, yes. Now hurry home so I can pick you up and do you against the wall."

She laughed. "Please, like you could lift me."

"Oh, baby, challenge accepted." Giggling, she rolled her eyes, but inside she was elated. "See you soon. Love you."

"Love you too," she said before hanging up and laying her phone down. With the biggest grin on her face, she pulled the dress up and over her bump, zipping it up the side. When she looked back at herself, her grin didn't leave. She loved it. The lace was so elegant, and it fit great across her breasts, while hitting her right at midthigh. It fit her belly perfectly, which was always the hard part. There was beading, but not too much for people to assume it was a wedding dress. It was stunning.

She had the perfect blue and pink kimono that would go great over the top and downplay it a bit. With a nod, she decided this was it and went out to show Autumn.

Autumn was waiting, and when she saw Baylor, her eyes lit up. "Oh, I love it."

"It's almost nineteen hundred dollars," Baylor said dryly, fully expecting to pay for it herself.

"So? It's perfect," Autumn said sternly before popping off the tag and walking away.

"Aw, you look beautiful, Baylor," Avery gushed, holding Ashlyn in her arms as she wiggled to get down.

"Yes, I love it!" Claire declared, and when she grinned over at Lucy, Baylor felt like something was up.

"It's perfect," Lucy said, and Baylor eyed her.

"For a baby shower?"

"Yes," Lucy said slowly, and then she turned, leaving quickly.

Yeah, something was up.

But Baylor was more concerned with getting home.

To the challenge her husband had accepted.

A Sinclair Baby Shower

The baby shower for Baylor and Jayden was completely over-the-top.

Autumn had gone above and beyond, but if Baylor was honest, she loved it.

It was at dusk, and the sun was slowly going down, which gave such a romantic feel to the party in Jayden and Baylor's backyard. Instead of lots of pink and blue, Autumn had done gold and white. Everything was sparkling and not Baylor at all, but in a way, it was perfect. Each table was covered in a huge arrangement of white peonies that had gold painted bottles and spoons in them. Balloons filled with gold glitter were everywhere, and above the cake—which was four layers of cheesecake, Baylor's biggest craving—were balloons that spelled out *Congratulations J&B.*

Standing in the middle of the baby shower with Jayden holding her waist, Baylor all of a sudden started crying.

"Oh, God," Jayden said, shaking his head, but Baylor couldn't help it. "What is wrong? You said you loved it."

"I've never seen anything so beautiful," she cried, which had him breaking out into a burst of laughter.

Turning her so she faced him, he wrapped his arms around her, kissing her lips and then her forehead. His kisses were like a drug, a beautiful drug she wanted to overuse. Pulling back, he looked deep into her eyes, his green ones shining with love as he whispered, "I say that every time I see you."

With her lip puckered out, she stared up into his eyes as he slowly wiped her face free of tears, kissing her hard on the lips. Sinking into the kiss, she let go, her tears falling again and her heart filling with such love. She hadn't wanted this party; she hadn't wanted to be paraded around as the big fat lady at a party full of her friends and family. But now, in Jayden's arms, his lips pressed to hers, she didn't want to be anywhere else.

Pulling back, she looked up into his beautiful eyes, her own eyes flooding with tears. "I could say the same about you. I don't know of many people who wear suits to a baby shower, but you wear it well, Mr. Sinclair."

He nodded, shrugging his shoulders as he dusted them off. "I know. Thought since you were going to look so incredible, I had to keep up. Though, I'm lacking beside you, baby."

She giggled happily as she leaned into him. "I beg to differ."

He went to say something, mischief in his eyes, but then someone pushed Jayden away.

"Get your hands off my best friend," Markus said, wrapping his arms around her and kissing her cheek.

Crying out in joy, she wrapped her arms around him, hugging him tightly as he lifted her only slightly off the ground. She hadn't seen him in months since he'd moved to Florida, and he wasn't supposed to be here.

"I thought you couldn't come!" she gushed, pulling back to look down into his dark caramel eyes.

"You think I'd miss today? No way. I'm staying for the week, so you better drop this kid while I'm here so he can meet his uncle Markus," he said, hugging her tightly before setting her on her feet. "Man, you look amazing. And all the glowing shit, it's true. I didn't realize you were so big, though. You've been

taking good selfies for Facebook."

Glaring, she smacked him. "I hate you."

"I love you too!" he said, kissing her once more.

"I can't believe you're here. I'm so happy," Baylor exclaimed, and he grinned back at her.

"I know. Thank your hunky husband, he demanded I be here. Paid for it and all, you know, because I'm a poor little hockey player in the AHL."

Baylor rolled her eyes. "Whatever. You just blew all your money."

"That too," he agreed, and Baylor couldn't stop grinning. "But yeah, I'm excited and ready for this baby to get here."

"Me too. Did you bring anyone?" she asked, and he scoffed.

"Please, we both know I fucked that up," he reminded her, and Baylor nodded. It wasn't like her best friend to cheat, but he had, and because of it, he'd lost the one girl he really loved. Though it had taken losing her for him to realize it. "But that is the last thing I want to talk about," he said before bringing Jayden back over to the conversation. "You can have her back. I gotta go see your mom and her dad."

"Thanks, asshole," Jayden teased, and Markus grinned.

"But, hey, Sinclair," he said as he slowly backed away and Jayden took her in his arms, kissing her temple.

"Yeah?"

"I'm completely jealous of you right now," he said, and Baylor grinned. There wasn't any kind of anything between the two of them, but it was still really great to hear.

When Markus turned his back on them, she looked up to her husband and smiled. "You are the best husband in the world."

Grinning, Jayden nodded. "I know."

"No, really, you didn't have to bring him in for me."

"Yeah, I did. I knew you wanted him here," he said simply, moving her hair behind her ear before running his hands down her braid and then down her side.

"Thank you," she whispered before going on her toes to kiss his jaw. As she pulled back, she said, "I love—"

But she was interrupted when Autumn came up to them. "Hey, Baylor, can you come with me real quick?"

Looking to her mother-in-law, Baylor's brows came together. "Yeah, I guess…"

But before she could even finish, Autumn was dragging her away. Grinning back at Baylor, Jayden said, "See you in a few."

Confused, she walked into their guesthouse, or more accurately, she was pushed into the guesthouse before Autumn shut the door quickly. Turning to Baylor, Autumn said, "Take off the kimono."

"Huh?" she asked, but Autumn was already removing it before handing her a big bouquet of peonies. "What in the world am I supposed to do with this?"

Before Autumn could answer, though, a knock came to the door, and she opened it.

Baylor's father, River, popped his head in and asked, "Ready?"

"Ready?"

"Yes," Autumn said, kissing Baylor's cheek and then leaving her with River.

"Dad? What in the world is going on?"

Her father had a happy little grin on his face as he held out his arm to her. "Why don't you come on out here with me?"

"Okay, but why?" she asked, feeling like something was going on.

Reaching for her, he laughed as he tucked her arm in his. "You know I love you and I'm proud of you, right, Little Fifty?" he asked, his eyes misting as he used Baylor's nickname.

Watching her father, she slowly nodded. "I thought I was supposed to be the emotional one? I'm the one having the baby, Dad."

"I know, and I'm so proud of you."

"Thanks…? I'm so confused about what's going on," she said, her eyes

widening. "Wait, are you dying?"

He laughed. "No, come on," he said, pulling her out the door, and when she looked out into the yard, everyone was looking back at her in an almost circular shape. In the middle was Jayden, standing with an older man she was pretty sure was the pastor of his family's church. The same person who had married their parents.

What in the world?

Clearing his throat, Jayden held her gaze as his face curved in a grin. "Baylor, I fell in love with you three years ago. I'll never forget the moment I saw you." Baylor couldn't move; she was trapped in his gaze. "I was on the beach with my bonehead brothers—"

"Hey, I'm amazing. Jace is a bonehead," Jude said, and Jace scoffed.

"Other way around, buddy."

"Like I said, boneheads," Jayden reiterated, and everyone laughed, but no one looked away. Though, who could? He was beautiful. "I saw you standing with the girl my brother was hitting on, and I was just captivated by you. Completely and utterly stunned, but then you challenged me in hockey. Only wearing short shorts and a tank top, but you didn't care. You threw on a pair of skates, and you swept the floor with me. I think that's the moment I fell for you."

The tears were there before she could even try to stop them.

"Things didn't work out at first, and even more so when I found out you were the daughter of my new coach, but I never stopped loving you. When you pushed me away, I pushed back, needing you to love me as much as I loved you. When you finally gave in, I knew I had won it all, that nothing could top the way I felt. But you proved me wrong," he said, pausing as he looked away, moving his hand over his mouth before sucking in a deep breath. "You married me," he said, his voice breaking when he looked back at her. "And now you're carrying my baby. I don't think you know what that does to me, how I fall for you over and over again, each day. I couldn't do this thing called life without you, Baylor Irene Moore Sinclair, and I know I didn't give you the wedding you deserve. That I didn't give your dad the chance to give you away or to have the pictures of us from that day on the wall. So, I've got a question," he said, but it was hard to listen because she was sobbing like a damn baby.

"Yeah?" she croaked out, and everyone was grinning at her. There wasn't a dry eye in the crowd that had gathered in her backyard. Autumn was crying as she held Angie close to her, while the rest of family smiled back at Baylor, all of them holding on to the ones they loved. Their friends, a group consisting of all the Assassins, were there, all with tears in their eyes as they watched Baylor cry. Usually, she would be embarrassed, but all she saw was Jayden, grinning at her with all the love and admiration in the world in his eyes.

Only for her.

"Will you marry me, again? Right here, with all our friends and family as witnesses and your dad giving you away?"

She didn't even pause or think, she just beamed, nodding like a fool. "You don't even have to ask."

"Oh, really? I never know with you. Wasn't sure if you hated me today."

"Never," she said as she started to pull her dad along, but Jayden held his hand up to her.

"No, wait. I have the greatest singer/songwriter ever on hand to sing as you walk down the aisle," he said. He looked to Avery, but she was crying on Jace.

Looking up at Jayden, Avery groaned, "Dude, I'm crying here."

"So? I paid you, get out here," he demanded, and soon the tears turned to laughter as Avery dragged her guitar with her over to the chair that was waiting for her.

"Jeez, he's mean," she said to Baylor, wiping her face.

"He's the best," Baylor said, and Jayden sent her a grin that could light up an arena.

Running her fingers along the chords, Avery looked up as she started to play "The One" by Kodaline.

Their song.

A song that to that day still gave Baylor chills and butterflies. Her lip started to wobble, and within seconds, more tears were rushing down her face. She was pretty sure she was about to run out of them. "You suck," she called to Jayden, and he chortled a bit.

"Hey, we can't do this without our song," he said as she and her dad started to walk to him. It was a short walk, but they walked slowly because she wanted to hear the whole song. "Plus, I love watching you cry."

"'Cause you're sadistic," she said. Everyone laughed because, really, how silly were they?

"No, it's 'cause I'm watching you. Everything about you, I love."

Breathless, she leaned into her father as she swooned completely. For a quiet man, Jayden really knew what to say to make her swoon like a schoolgirl. When Baylor finally reached him, Jayden held his hand out to River, which he quickly took, shaking it hard.

"Thank you for this, Jayden," her father said, his voice a little rough. Jayden nodded, but her father didn't let go of his hand. "I should hate you. I mean, you ran off with her, married her before you two's draft celebration dinner. I had no say, I wasn't even there, but you know what I felt?"

River's eyes were locked on his as Jayden said, "No, sir, I don't."

River nodded. "I was proud. I was stunned, for obvious reasons, but I wasn't upset. I was happy. Because not only was my daughter living her dream, she had found the greatest man ever to live it with," he said sternly, and from behind her, Baylor heard Autumn choke on a sob. "I have considered you a son for a very long time, and I am truly blessed to see the man you have grown into. Lord knows, I thank the big man upstairs for you every day because I don't worry about her at all. I know my baby is protected and loved. And I know for a fact the baby that is coming is about to have the greatest father in the world. Because of that, I thank you, and I want you to know I love you, son."

River then let Baylor go, taking Jayden in his arms and hugging him tightly. When he pulled back, they both smacked each other's biceps before River reached for Baylor's hand, handing it to Jayden. Choking back her own sob, she turned to her husband and felt nothing but pure wonder for the man who was her forever.

"Ready?" he asked, lacing his fingers with hers.

"I'll always be ready to marry you," she said, squeezing his hand.

"Again?"

"Over and over again, I don't care, as long as it's you."

As Jayden grinned back at her, his eyes were misty. But before he could say anything, Jude called out, "Lord, get on with it. Y'all are giving us all a sugar rush!"

"Jude Marshall, shut your mouth!" Autumn yelled, but all Baylor could do was grin back at Jayden.

Her forever.

And just like the day she married him the first time, she remembered her list of goals.

Make it into the NHL. Check.

Make her dad proud. Check. Double check.

Find the love of her life. Check.

Tell him she loved him every day. A billion times checked.

Win the Stanley Cup. No check, but she didn't need it.

Jayden would always be the biggest trophy of her life.

And even though "Have a baby" was never on that list, it was now, and she couldn't wait to mark it as checked.

Did you just piss on me?

ell, that was so sugary sweet, I'm pretty sure I got a toothache," Markus said as he fell back on Baylor's couch. "Or it was all the cheesecake I ate."

Baylor giggled as Jayden brought her down onto his lap, his hand resting on her belly. The party was over, and Baylor was convinced it was one of the greatest days of her life. The impromptu wedding was amazing and so romantic. She hadn't expected it, and she had to admit, she was really starting to love surprises. Well, as long as they included Jayden.

After they redid their vows, they danced as Avery sang "This" by Ed Sheeran. After that, they opened presents, and it was easy to say their child would be set for the first year of its life. It would definitely be ready for its first hockey game in its stylish Number 59 Sinclair Assassins jersey Elli had gotten them. Along with the Assassins blanket, hat, pacifier, and carrier. They had gotten so much stuff—even a stick and puck for the little baby. She just couldn't wait to find a home for every gift.

But she was more ready for the baby to come.

"Hush, it was amazing," she gushed, kissing Jayden's cheek as he peeled off her shoes, rubbing her feet.

"You loved it?"

"I did," she said, cuddling into him. "Did your mom plan it?"

"Nope, all me," he said proudly, and she beamed back at him.

"Wow, good move, Sinclair. It was nice," Markus said with a nod. "Way better than those stupid shower games."

Baylor laughed. "Right? But it was all perfect, and I can't wait to put all the stuff away."

"Do I have to help?" Markus asked, and Jayden scoffed.

"If I have to fold onesies, so do you," he said, and Markus nodded.

"Figured. Gotta work for the plane ticket, I guess," he teased, and they all had a good laugh.

Leaning against Jayden, she looked up at the wall that was empty, waiting for what she had thought would be pictures of their child. "I want the pictures there."

Jayden looked at the spot she was pointing to, his brows coming together. "I thought the baby's first pictures were going there."

"Nope, I want pictures of us, with the baby in the middle."

"Anything you want," he whispered, kissing her temple, and Markus groaned.

"You guys are mushy. Ew," he teased, a grin pulling at his lips, and Baylor stuck her tongue out.

"You're jealous."

"I am. Can I move in and be the third wheel? I'm lonely."

"No way," Jayden laughed, looking over to their friend. "So it's not going well down in Florida?"

"Hate it. Loathe it. I want to leave. Y'all are up here, and Jace is all the way in Ft. Lauderdale. I don't have anything in common with my team. I hate it."

"You'll be brought up, just give it time. Not everyone goes straight in," Jayden said, and Markus nodded.

"I know. I'm just impatient and bored."

"Try being me. I've played hockey my whole life, and now that's all gone. I'm growing a child, and I have no hockey. Things change in an instant. Don't give up," Baylor said, a smile on her face, and Markus beamed back at her, leaning into the couch cushions.

"And you're doing it effortlessly, babe. I wish I had y'all's life."

Looking at her husband, Baylor decided she did have a pretty great life. She just wished her best friend did too. He'd almost had it, but he'd thrown that away. Glancing back at Markus, she knew even though it was a sore subject, she had to ask. "You haven't talked to Mekena at all?"

He scoffed, shaking his head while not looking at her. "No, man. She wants nothing to do with me, not that I blame her."

"Yeah," she agreed. "But maybe—"

"Nah, no use."

"You know she'll be at Lucy and Benji's wedding?" Jayden asked. "She's the photographer, from what I heard Avery say to Mom."

"Yeah, that's what Jace said."

"Maybe you can talk to her, then," Baylor suggested, but Markus didn't look hopeful as his eyes met hers.

"It's been almost a year, Bay. I doubt she gives two shits about me or that she wants to. I'll get over her. I just need more time."

"Yeah," Baylor agreed as she shifted to the side from a pain that shot up her back all of a sudden. "Ack."

"What?"

"I got a pain."

"A pain?" Jayden was alarmed as he watched her. "What kind of pain?"

When it shot up her back once more, she cried out, gripping his shoulder while she sucked in a breath. "Pain, pain."

"Like, baby pain?" Markus asked, his eyes widening, concern filling them.

"I don't know," she wailed, her back on fire. Surely, it wasn't time. She wasn't ready. "It just hurts."

"Do we need to go in? Markus, grab her bag," Jayden said, but Baylor didn't move, leaning into him as her back seized up. It hurt, badly, but it was probably just Braxton-Hicks; she had them a lot. Though, this felt more intense. That scared her.

"I don't know. Wait, stop. Give me a minute. It's not time. I've got like two weeks."

She hissed out a breath, but Jayden was shaking his head. "Maybe we should call my mom, I doubt she's far."

"No, I'm fine—" But before she could even finish, a warmth rushed out of her, wetting her thighs.

Jayden cried out, "Shit, are you pissing on me?"

With her eyes wide, she shook her head. "No, I think my water broke."

"Oh, hell. Can you get up? Markus, get her bag. Shit, we gotta go," Jayden said frantically, helping Baylor up.

"Ew, gross. You've got baby juices on you," Markus said. But when Baylor looked up, he had the bag.

"Shut up, Markus," Jayden said as he held up his hand. "Let me change, and we'll leave. Is that okay? Can you wait?"

"Yeah, I'm fine. Let me change too," she said calmly as the pain lessened enough for her to stand, but Jayden didn't move. "I don't want to go soaked in baby juices."

"Maybe you should just stay there. You don't want to move too much, right?"

"It's fine."

"Why are you so calm? You're having a baby!" Markus cried out, as frantic as Jayden.

"Yeah, this isn't something to be so calm about. Where is emotional, crazy Baylor?"

She rolled her eyes, passing by Jayden. "I'm sure she'll rear her ugly head.

Until then, let's go get changed and head up to the hospital. These things can take forever from what I've heard, so I don't want to be just sitting there."

But that wasn't the case for Baylor. Because when they got to the hospital and in the bed for the doctor to check her, Jayden and Baylor were completely blown away when the doctor said, "Wow, you're at a six. This is going to be fast. Hope you're ready."

Baylor looked to Jayden, who looked to her, and they both laughed. "No, we aren't ready!" he said, shaking his head. "We haven't finished those birthing classes."

"The room is nowhere near ready."

"Did you install the baby seat?"

"No, I thought you had."

"Lord, we're a mess! I thought we had two more weeks," Jayden laughed, his face full of happiness. But his eyes told the truth; he was scared to death. Though, Baylor was sure she looked the same.

Because she was scared out of her mind.

"Well, it's coming. Might want to call family," Dr. Flynn said before taking off her glove and tapping Baylor's leg. "Want some pain meds?"

Baylor shook her head. "I want a natural birth."

When Markus hissed in shock, she smiled as he said, "Show-off."

Baylor laughed as Dr. Flynn nodded. "Sounds good to me. I'll be back in a few."

"Thanks," Baylor said before looking to Markus.

"Can you call Jace and Jude while Jayden calls Mom, Dad, and Lucy?"

"Yeah, but from now on, make sure I'm on this side of you. I just saw way more of you than I ever wanted," he said, making a face of pure horror, causing Baylor to giggle.

"So I guess you aren't going to hold my leg back?"

He looked up at her, alarmed. "Please don't make me do that."

Holding back her giggle, she smiled. "But I was depending on you."

Looking to Jayden for help, Markus found none since he was on the phone. "You're joking."

"Yeah, I am. Jayden's mom is going to be in here."

"Thank God," he breathed as he pulled out his phone, calling the rest of the family.

Looking up at the ceiling, she felt her body start to seize up once more. Like she had been practicing, she did the breathing techniques that had gotten her to this moment. She was scared. Would she be able to handle the real pain? Maybe she should get the pain meds… But ever since she had found out she was pregnant and she'd already been taking meds for her knee, she had promised herself she would never take anything stronger than ibuprofen because she was scared she'd hurt the baby. No, she could do this.

She was strong.

She was woman; hear her roar.

"We got this," she said, looking to her husband, who was a nice shade of greenish-white. "We're gonna rock this birth. Kick its ass and get the greatest reward ever."

Jayden nodded, though not confidently at all. She could see it in his eyes. He was freaking out. "Okay, yeah. Yeah, we are."

"Don't worry, it will go easy and well. I just know it."

With his brows to his hairline, he said, "Never expected you to be calm and cool about this."

She scoffed. "Right. Usually, you're the calm one."

"Yeah," he said with a grin. "But you're right. We got this."

She held up her hand for a high five. "Damn right. Let's do this, Sinclair."

Slapping her hand, he laced his fingers with hers before kissing her hard on the lips. "You are fucking amazing, and I love you."

Grinning like a fool, Baylor nodded. "I love you too, now let's make this birth our bitch."

As confident as she was an hour before, though, nothing could prepare

her for the pain when it really started up. The sounds she was making were something straight out of a horror film. It was so bad, Markus had to leave the room, unable to watch his best friend in such pain. Poor Jayden was white as a sheet as he held her hand, telling her how beautiful she was, how strong she was.

"I don't think I can do this," she cried, leaning into his hand as the pain took over, making her delirious.

"Yes, you can. I know you can. You can do anything," he promised in her ear, moving the washcloth along her head as the door opened and Autumn hustled in.

"I'm so sorry! We were already home, my damn phone was off, and Lord! I'm so sorry!"

"It's fine, Mom. She's at eight."

"Wow, moving along," Autumn said, coming to the other side of the bed and moving her hand along Baylor's arm. "We're gonna have us a baby soon."

"Thank God," Baylor struggled to say as she leaned into Jayden's hand, squeezing it so hard she was sure she was going to break it off.

"Everyone is in the waiting room. They wanted to me to tell you they love you and are so proud of you guys. And Lord knows your daddy can't stand to see you in pain," Autumn said, but all Baylor could do was cry out as the pain once again took over.

"Keep breathing, baby, you're doing awesome."

"Ugh, it hurts so bad," she cried out, reaching for Autumn's outstretched hand and squeezing. "Fuck. Damn it. Ugh, this sucks!"

"I know, honey. It will be worth it, don't worry. Just keep breathing," Autumn encouraged, but Baylor wasn't sure it would ever end—or that she would make it. It just hurt. Everything hurt. But then, all of a sudden, she needed to push.

"Fuck, I gotta push now. Jayden, now!" she yelled, squeezing their hands. Within seconds, a nurse was in the room, her hand up inside of Baylor, checking her.

"Yup, it's baby time," she said, and Baylor let out a harsh breath as tears ran down her face.

"See, baby? It's time. You've done so great," Jayden said, kissing her temple and cheek. "Almost there. Are you ready? Ready to meet our little baby?"

Nodding, she really didn't want to cuss him out, but he had to stop talking to her. "Not now. I love you, Jayden Mitchell Sinclair, I do. But right now, I want to kill you. So just hold my hand and tell me I'm pretty as I push your kid out."

The room filled with laughter as the doctor came in, getting dressed while Jayden nodded. "Yes, ma'am. God, you're so pretty."

Everything was happening so fast. She heard the click of a phone, and when she looked up to Autumn, she was taking pictures. Great. They'd need those, but the pain was almost pure hell. Burning. That's all Baylor felt.

"All right, Baylor, next contraction, we're doing this."

"Okay," she agreed, bringing her legs back as Jayden and Autumn both grabbed a knee.

"You got this, baby," Jayden said, his head leaned against hers as the contraction hit and Baylor pushed with everything in her soul.

"Whoa, great pushing!" the doctor encouraged, but it was hard to hear her over the pure fucking fire Baylor was feeling. Closing her eyes, she cried out as another contraction came, and she pushed once more. "We have a head. Do you wanna feel the head, Baylor?"

"No, I fucking want it out!" she screamed, her body feeling as if it wasn't even hers.

"Holy shit, Baylor. It's right there. You're almost there," Jayden cried, and she wanted to appreciate his enthusiasm, she did, but not right now.

"Well, if the baby has shoulders like you, I'm fucked," she grunted as another contraction hit, and she started pushing once more. The baby apparently did have shoulders like its father because it took several more pushes until, finally, the cries of her baby filled the room.

"It's a boy!" the doctor exclaimed.

"Oh my God," Jayden cried out.

Autumn bubbled a sob, but all Baylor could do was cry as the doctor lifted the baby, putting him on her stomach for her to see.

And boy, what a scary little thing he was.

Big as all get-out, with blood and fluids covering every inch of him, and a full head of hair. She was pretty sure he had Jayden's nose and chin, but as he screamed in sheer frustration, Baylor figured that was all her.

And just like that, Baylor was in love.

Still unable to speak, she just moved her finger along his head as Jayden cut the cord, his tears coming down his face in sheets.

"Baby, you did it," he cried, kissing her over and over again. "I'm so proud of you."

Looking up at him, she beamed. "We did it."

"You did it."

Gasping for breath, she kissed her little boy's head. She felt so dizzy, so out of breath, but she was pretty sure that was normal.

"So, what do you think? Rhett or Dawson? You said you'd know when you saw him."

She had said that, but she couldn't think right now. Closing her eyes, she sucked in a breath, but she still felt like she couldn't catch it. She felt wrong. Everything was spinning. Something was wrong.

"Jayd—"

And then, it was black.

God, it's Jayden Sinclair. Take me instead.

"Code Blue, she's crashing. I can't stop the bleeding."

Completely confused, Jayden looked up from his beautiful boy to the doctor who was still between his wife's legs.

What?

"Clamps. Get them out of here," Dr. Flynn said, and when Jayden looked up to Baylor, he saw her head listing to the side, her eyes closed as the medical staff hurried to get the baby off her before rushing to get oxygen on her.

Everything stopped. "Baylor? Baylor! Are you okay? Baby?" he cried, reaching for her, shaking her a bit, but she wasn't moving. Was she even breathing? But before he could make sure, he was being ushered away.

"Baylor? What happened? Honey! Wake up," Autumn cried, holding Baylor's face. But then someone grabbed her too, pushing them both out the door.

"Sir, we need you to wait outside," a nurse said, but he struggled, trying to get away.

"No! What is going on?"

"She's bleeding, and the doctor needs to get it to stop. Please, don't fight

me. Just wait," she said, finally getting him out. But as he went to go back in, the door shut in his face.

"I'm sure it's fine, Jayden. It has to be fine," his mother said, her voice trembling as he stared at the door, the noises of doctors and nurses working coming through it, along with the sounds of his son's cries.

"She needs me," he whispered as Autumn took him in her arms, holding him close.

"Let them work on her. It's fine," she said once more.

But seconds turned to minutes and still no word. Baylor had to be okay. He couldn't do life without her. People didn't die during childbirth anymore, did they? He really should have read that damn book Baylor told him to read. Closing his eyes, he covered them as he sucked in a deep breath, trying to calm his heart and his breathing. Though, it didn't work.

Finally, the door opened, but it was only for a nurse to bring out his son.

His son. That should please him to no end, but he was shaking with fear for his wife.

Racing the short distance to the nurse who was pushing his son in his little bassinette, he stopped her. But she shut the door before he could get around her. "My wife, is she okay?"

"I don't know, sir. They're going to be out in a moment," she said, but she wouldn't look him in the eye. "Would you like to come with the baby?"

"I need to know about my wife. Mom," he said, turning to his mother, but she was already there.

"Of course. I'll go."

"Okay," the nurse said, still not looking Jayden in the eye, and that did nothing but fill him with dread. Standing alone in the busy hall, aware he was slowly but surely dying inside, Jayden wasn't certain he'd made the right decision. Should he have gone with the baby? No. He needed to know about Baylor.

When the door opened, he had to take a step back as a nurse backed out, pulling Baylor's bed with her. "Baylor," he gasped, and when he saw the blood-soaked sheets, he cried out. "Oh God, is she okay?"

But none of the nurses answered him.

They just wheeled her as Dr. Flynn came out, pausing in front of him. "Doc, tell me something. Anything. Is she okay?"

"I don't know yet. She's lost a lot of blood. We were able to get the placenta out, but she won't stop bleeding. So we are taking her to the OR for a transfusion and to see if there is a tear in the uterus or vagina that's causing the bleeding. It could be a number of things, but I won't know which until I'm there."

All he heard was she'd lost a lot of blood.

"Will she be okay?"

"Jayden, I'm sorry, but I can't answer that. Let me go work on her."

She went to go around him, but he stopped her. "Please, I need her. She's my life."

Dr. Flynn's eyes widened, and she nodded. "I know. I'm doing everything I can."

"Can I come?"

"No, I'm sorry. You need to wait here."

Moving past him, she ran down the hall, leaving Jayden with no promises at all. Swallowing hard, he covered his face as he walked backward into the wall, the hard surface giving him the support he needed. The fear of losing his wife took over his body. He couldn't fathom what had just happened. Why was this happening? He loved her; she loved him. They were good people, donated to charity, went to church, and above all, they loved Jesus. They were so excited, and they had been through so much. Why? Why was this happening?

Squeezing his eyes shut, he whispered, "Please, Lord, take me instead. Take me. Don't take her. I need her. *We* need her. My son and I. Please."

He waited, needing some kind of sign, but none came.

"Jay, bro, you okay?"

Lifting his head, he saw Jude and Jace racing toward him, Markus on their

heels. "Mom texted from the nursery. Told us what was going on. Are you okay?"

He couldn't even answer them. He just fell into Jude, and thankfully, his brother caught him, wrapping his arms around him. He held him tight as Jayden let go, his sobs filling the hall.

"They don't know what's wrong. She won't stop bleeding," he cried, and then he felt Jace's and Markus's hands on his back.

"It's fine, she'll be fine. Baylor is the strongest girl I know. It's okay, just breathe, bro. It's fine," Jude said, his own voice frantic as he held Jayden.

"Where is she?" Markus asked, and Jayden shook his head, backing away from Jude as he sucked in a breath, looking down at the floor.

"In the OR."

No one said anything. They stood there awkwardly, waiting for something or someone to tell them what to do. He could feel everyone's anxiety, his own most of all. Usually, he was the strong one. The pillar of the family. But right now, he was doing everything he could to stay upright and not fall to his knees to beg the Lord to protect his wife, to keep her here.

Finally, a nurse came up to him, her face full of worry. "Mr. Sinclair, there is a waiting room by the OR you can wait in."

"Is she okay? My wife, Baylor Sinclair?"

"I don't know, sir. Please follow me," she said, looking away, and it felt off. Why couldn't they just say if Baylor was okay? If she was going to be okay?

He couldn't think that way. She was okay. She would be fine.

Together, the guys walked to the surgery waiting room, and while Jace and Markus sat with the rest of the family who had relocated from the maternity ward waiting room, Jayden stood by the door with Jude right beside him. He had a perfect view of the door to the OR from where he stood, and he wasn't moving until he knew if his wife was okay. Looking back to Jude, he swallowed hard. Jude wasn't the serious type, but he looked as stricken as Jayden felt.

Fighting back the tears, Jayden leaned his head against the door and said,

"My boy is gorgeous."

Jude nodded, his hand coming to his brother's shoulder. "I heard."

"I didn't go with him. Does that make me a bad father?"

"No, it makes you a great one 'cause you're protecting his momma."

Jayden slowly nodded, the tears flooding his eyes. When River came running into the waiting room, his eyes wild with worry, Jayden couldn't look at him, feeling completely worthless in front of the man whose daughter he had promised to protect.

Breathless, River said, "My boy, it's okay. We're okay. She's okay."

"I couldn't protect her. I failed you," Jayden whispered, and that made River come undone, taking Jayden in a back-slapping hug.

"She's fine. Don't worry. Hey," River said, backing up and shaking Jayden until he looked back at him. "She is fine, and you haven't, nor will you ever, fail me. It's okay. She's gonna be fine. We have to believe that," he says as sternly as he could through his sobs.

"He's right. Baylor's got this," Markus said on a sigh, and Jayden nodded.

"What happened? Autumn really didn't know."

Jayden shrugged as he explained, feeling completely useless. "They told us to wait here."

"No word, then?"

"None."

"Okay, so we wait."

But none of them was ready to wait as long as they had to. None of them left Jayden, though. River and Jude stood beside him by the door, while Jace, Avery, Ashlyn, Claire, Lucy, Benji, Angie, and Markus sat in the chairs against the wall, all of them silent as they waited for anything—anyone to tell them what was going on.

"Should I go check on the baby? Do you think he is okay?" Jayden asked then, worried for his boy but still terrified for his wife.

"Autumn said he is fine, healthy, a big old nine pounds, seven ounces.

Hockey player, that one is," River said, but even though he was trying to act strong, his voice was miserable. "Cute little thing. Obviously takes after Baylor."

Jayden smiled. "Obviously. She's the most gorgeous creature on this planet."

"She is," her father agreed as Jayden's eyes fell shut, his heart breaking in his chest. His head was aching, and everything weighed on him a billion times heavier than ever. He couldn't shake the thought she wasn't going to make it. He wanted to be optimistic, but why hadn't they said anything? Why hadn't they reassured him?

He was losing it.

"But she didn't even get to name him. What do I do? I can't name him. I suck at naming things. I named my dog, Dog, because I couldn't come up with anything else," Jayden said, frantically looking at each person, his heart in his throat.

"Dude, she'll name him. Don't worry," Jace said, holding his older brother's gaze. "It's going to be okay."

"Okay," he said, trying to catch his breath, but he still felt he was losing it all.

Sliding down the door, he sat on his haunches, covering his face as he breathed in and out hard, thinking, *Please, Lord. Take me. Please. Just take me. She's gotta raise this baby. I'll suck without her. I need her. Please. A son needs his momma, he does. Please.*

When Jude was back at his side, his hand on Jayden's back, Jayden's tears came faster. "I don't know what I will do."

"You don't have to think about that, bro. She's going to be fine," Jude promised, his eyes full of the hope Jayden was lacking.

"And if not?" he whispered, his whole body breaking out in sweat.

"Then as a family, we'll raise him. Don't you worry. Everything will be fine."

But a world without Baylor wasn't a world at all.

At least, not for Jayden and his son.

Swallowing hard, he looked up right as the door opened and Dr. Flynn walked out, wearing a fresh pair of scrubs and wiping her forehead. He stood up quickly as the doctor walked to him, letting out a long breath.

"Doc," Jayden croaked out, and she nodded. "Please give me something."

"Jayden, she is stable. We were able to replace the blood, stop the bleeding, and she is going to be just fine."

Crying out, he covered his eyes as River wrapped his arms around him, hugging Jayden tightly, his own sobs leaving his lips. *Thank you, Lord.*

Opening his eyes, Jayden swallowed back his sob as he nodded. "Thank you. So much."

"Of course. I'm sorry I couldn't give you more at first, but it just happened so quickly, and my only priority was to save her."

"And she is okay?"

"Yes, she'll heal fine. We'll monitor her once she's released for about the next month or so, but I feel good about it."

"Thank you," he said once more, breathing in hard as his tears ran down his face. "When can I see her?"

"She's in recovery for another twenty minutes, and then they'll take her to her room. She was asking for the baby and you when she finally came out of the anesthesia. So maybe you can go get him and meet her in there?"

Jayden smiled, nodding his head. "Good plan. Thank you again."

Dr. Flynn nodded, and as everyone thanked her, Jayden left to go get his son.

He had a smile on his face and happiness in his heart.

His family was safe and healthy.

So this is love?

Baylor felt high as hell, but she was eager to see her baby.

Looking around the room, she still felt a little weak and awfully tired, but she hated the silence. She wanted Jayden. She wanted her baby. Closing her eyes, she took in a breath, thankful she had survived. It had happened so fast. One moment, she was there, the next, she'd passed out. The vessels that held her placenta had ruptured, and then she was hemorrhaging. Baylor had lost a lot of blood, which resulted in the transfusions and the emergency surgery of her uterus, where Dr. Flynn had found and fixed the problem. Baylor was sure Jayden had been freaking out, and that scared her most of all. She didn't want him worrying about her. Though, she knew he was.

She just wanted to see him.

When she heard the door creak, her eyes flew open to see her father and Markus coming into the room. "Hey."

"Hey, you," her father said, coming to her side and taking her hand in his. Leaning down, he kissed her temple as Markus rubbed her thigh. "You gave us one hell of a scare."

"You sure as hell did. Don't do that again," Markus said, a smile on his lips.

49

"Who's gonna boss us around if you're not here?"

Baylor grinned. "I'm sorry. Where is Jayden, my baby?"

"Coming," River answered, kissing the back of her hand. "That poor boy was stricken."

"I'm sure," she agreed. "I feel horrible."

"It isn't your fault," Markus said, giving her a small smile. "It just happened. He was just lost, though. I am pretty sure I've never seen him cry so much in life, and I watched that sugary sweet wedding last night."

That made Baylor smile as her father chuckled. "Yeah, so know that boy loves you."

"Oh, I know that," she said softly, just as the door opened once more. She couldn't see past her father and Markus, but then at the end of the bed appeared her husband with a blue bundle in his arms.

"If I didn't love this little guy so much, I'd drop him to hold you," he said, his eyes holding Baylor's as they filled with tears.

"Well, come here. Let me hold him, and you can hold us both." She decided, and then he was moving and doing just as she suggested. As her son cuddled deep into her arms, Jayden climbed into the bed, taking her in his. When she heard the door shut, she looked up to see her father and Markus had snuck out. She was thankful. She needed it to be just her and her boys right then.

Turning to look at Jayden, her eyes full of tears, she cried, "I'm so sorry."

"Don't be. Just look at this little guy."

She smiled. "He's perfect."

He nodded. "Yup, ten fingers and toes, and he's hung. He'll thank me later."

Sputtering with laughter, she rolled her eyes. "Freaking nerd."

Leaning into her, he kissed her temple, his nose ghosting across her cheek as he breathed her in. "Baylor, I've never been so scared in my entire life."

"I know. I'm sorry."

"Stop that. Just know that I prayed for God to take me, so... I might die."

Looking up at him, she blinked back her tears. "You did?"

"Yeah, no hesitations. I need you."

"Jayden."

"No, really, there was no other option. This world is nothing without you. Looking at y'all now, I'm pretty sure I'll never love anything as much as I love you and him."

Leaning her head to his, she nodded. "Same here."

Pressing her lips to his, she felt her eyes drift shut, and she knew she was completely whole.

Maybe a little weak and tired, but whole.

Pulling back, he kissed her nose before they both looked down as their baby let out a small whimper. He looked just like Jayden the more she looked at him, and she was all right with that. Just another reason to love the little guy even more, and boy, did she. After everything she had been through—the hell-driven pregnancy and the even more nightmarish birth—Elli was right, she had forgotten it all. All Baylor cared about was this perfect baby.

Moving her fingertip along his delicate nose, she and Jayden both smiled when he wrinkled his nose, moving away. "I can't believe he is here."

"Me either," Jayden agreed, reaching for his tiny hand and bringing it to his lips for a soft kiss. "He's everything I dreamed of."

"Me too."

Sharing a smile, Jayden gave her a kiss on the nose before pulling back and asking, "Okay, you need to name him because I was lost. So, which is it? Dawson or Rhett?"

Looking back to their bundle of perfection, she exhaled loudly. "Dawson."

He nodded. "I thought so too. Dawson River Sinclair."

She grinned up at him, and her eyes sparkled. "My dad will love that."

"Good strong hockey name, too."

"He has some big skates to fill," she said, her heart exploding in her chest.

"Yup, especially if he is going to wear number fifty," he said, and when she looked up, his eyes were full of tears. "I personally know that number was worn by the most amazing player I've ever known. And if he is going to wear it, he'd better be ready to win, just like his momma did."

Choking back her sob, she nodded. "Yeah, he better be." Looking down at their baby, she said, "You hear that, Dawson? You are a winner, little man. Don't ever forget that."

Leaning his head to hers, Jayden sighed loudly, moving his finger along Dawson's face. "I thought I knew what love was, but after almost losing you and meeting this little guy, I'm pretty sure I was mistaken."

Baylor grinned. "Yeah, I couldn't agree more."

Looking up at her, Jayden reached out, taking her face and moving his finger along her bottom lip. "So, Mrs. Sinclair, I have a question for you."

"And I have an answer."

"Good," he said, his lips pausing in the middle of her mouth. "Are you ready for this thing called life? 'Cause I can't do it without you."

With a grin on her lips and her arms full of as much love as was in her heart, she nodded. "Yes, 'cause I'm not going to let you do it with anyone but me and this little guy."

"Awesome, since that's how I planned my life, anyway." Grinning back at her, Jayden pressed his lips to hers, and Baylor was lost.

Lost in the pure love Jayden gave her constantly.

And she wouldn't have it any other way.

Her husband's lips pressed to hers and her baby in her arms.

What a beautiful addition to her forever.

The End

Made in the USA
Lexington, KY
06 July 2019